The Power of Journaling:
A Guided Pathway to Insight

Nicolle Napier-Ionascu, Psy.D.
Andrea Michelle Napier, MFA

The Power of Journaling:
A Guided Pathway to Insight

Copyright © 2013

www.drnicolleionascu.com

Nicolle Napier-Ionascu, Psy.D. - Author
Andrea Michelle Napier, MFA - Author
Annie Barbarika - Graphic Designer

Published in 2013 by:

Half Full Press
1814 Franklin Street, Suite 603
Oakland, CA 94612
(888) 612-9908

10 9 8 7 6 5 4 3 2 1

ISBN 978-0-9855036-1-1

Printed and bound in China.

Introduction

Dysfunctional relationships, boring jobs, weight problems, addiction. Making bad choice after bad choice. Wanting to change, but not knowing how. These are the issues that millions of people face every day—simply because of lack of insight. Lack of insight about one's behavior leads to feeling stuck in life. The power of journaling and taking a moment of daily self-reflection has proven to decrease anxiety and improve overall mental wellness. This book is meant to foster a type of journaling that hones into the specific need for the discovery of self and the world while incorporating aspects of fun and fantasy.

In pop culture, tests such as the Rorschach Inkblot Test are well-known and regularly referenced without a full appreciation for the brilliance of their projective techniques. In the world of psychology, a projective test—that is, an open-ended means of expression based on a reaction to a given prompt—provides a glimpse into behavior and emotions on a deeper level. Journaling, painting, and other means of daily artistic expression are wonderful ways to develop insight in the same way. It is time for people to stop being driven by feelings and conflicts that they cannot identify.

Insight is not a natural state of being for most individuals. Oftentimes people need help learning how to think about what they feel and the choices they make on a deeper level. Writing in a journal can be a daunting task because knowing how to get started is not easy. This journal provides a weekly prompt with subsequent daily questions to get the process of reflection started. Sometimes the prompts are simple complete-the-sentence formats, while others are more in-depth. Whatever the format, the prompts are inviting because humans are driven towards wanting to understand inner conflicts and motivations. As such, may this journal start a journey that leads to the peace that comes with a better understanding of the self.

About the Authors

Dr. Nicolle Napier-Ionascu, Psy.D.

Dr. Napier-Ionascu works as a clinical neuropsychologist in the department of neurology at Children's Hospital and Research Center in Oakland, CA. She is a contributing author for livestrong.com and ehow.com, having published over sixty articles for these sites in the past year.

Nicolle graduated from the University of California at Berkeley in the late 1990s with a degree in English Literature. She then went on to earn her Master's Degree and Doctorate in Clinical Psychology at the Wright Institute in Berkeley, specializing in Neuropsychology. While in graduate school, Nicolle conducted research examining interpersonal relationships, body image issues, and projective testing in young women, ultimately writing her dissertation on the role of such factors in personal development based on results of the Rorschach Inkblot Test.

Post doctoral fellowship and residency were completed at San Francisco General Hospital in the division of psychosocial medicine and neuropsychology within the University of San Francisco Medical School. Professionally, Nicolle began her post-educational career working on research involving cognitive retraining and methods of increasing insight in patients with schizophrenia at the VA Medical Center in San Francisco.

In 2007, during some time spent in North Carolina, Nicolle began writing for publications such as *Charlotte Parents Magazine* and the local newspaper *The County Edge*. Nicolle also joined the faculty of Queen's University at Charlotte.

Andrea Michelle Napier, MFA

After studying Fashion Design in London for a year, Ms. Napier returned to California to finish a Bachelor of Arts in Costume Design at California State University, Los Angeles. From there, she went on to receive a Master of Fine Arts in Costume Design from the University of Arizona, Tucson, where her emphasis was in Period Costume History and Construction.

Since graduation in 1995, Ms. Napier has been working in the Film and Television Industry as a Set Costumer in Wardrobe. Some of her more notable projects have been Power Rangers, Frasier, Starsky & Hutch, Span'glish, Brothers & Sisters, and currently Rizzoli & Isles.

Art and literature have always been a passion for Ms. Napier. She has had the pleasure of visiting some of the world's finest museums and marveled at their masterpieces in person. Ms. Napier is an avid reader of just about everything in print and is never comfortable without a book at her side.

Through writing and journaling, Ms. Napier has found an amazing outlet of expression and self-discovery that she hopes to share with others through this project.

Month One

Day 1 This photograph is all about point of view.
How would you describe this perspective?

....

....

....

....

....

....

....

....

....

....

....

Day 2 How do you view circumstances in your life as compared to this particular view?

....
....
....
....
....
....
....
....
....
....
....
....
....
....
....
....
....
....
....
....
....
....

Day 3 How can focus change the way you view a situation? Is this focus too narrow? Why or why not?

....
....
....
....
....
....
....
....
....
....
....
....
....
....
....
....
....
....
....
....
....
....

Day 4 Think about one thing this week that you viewed through a narrow focus and it was helpful. What were the circumstances?

....

....

....

....

....

....

....

....

....

....

....

....

....

....

....

....

....

....

....

....

Day 5 When can a wider focus help a situation?

....
....
....
....
....
....
....
....
....
....
....
....
....
....
....
....
....
....
....
....
....

Day 6 Is this perspective comfortable to you? Why or why not?

....
....
....
....
....
....
....
....
....
....
....
....
....
....
....
....
....
....
....
....

Day 7 Think about your week. Did you have a situation that you thought you viewed through a too narrow or too wide perspective?

....
....
....
....
....
....
....
....
....
....
....
....
....
....
....
....
....
....
....
....
....
....
....
....

"Look like the innocent flower, but be the serpent underneath it."

Day 1 What does an innocent flower look like in human form?

....

....

....

....

....

....

....

....

....

....

....

....

....

....

....

....

....

Day 2 Do you know anyone who lives up to this quote? Who?

....
....
....
....
....
....
....
....
....
....
....
....
....
....
....
....
....
....
....
....
....

Day 3 Who recently surprised you by seeming like an innocent flower, but was actually more like a serpent?

....
....
....
....
....
....
....
....
....
....
....
....
....
....
....
....
....
....
....

Day 4 Have you ever felt like a serpent? When?

....

....

....

....

....

....

....

....

....

....

....

....

....

....

....

....

....

....

....

Day 5 What kind of person would give this advice?

....

....

....

....

....

....

....

....

....

....

....

....

....

....

....

....

Notice how it feels to compare people to animals. If you are comfortable with using this imagery, you likely view people as having many complex layers to their personalities.

Day 6 Which would you rather be: the flower or the serpent? Why?

....

....

....

....

....

....

....

....

....

....

....

....

....

....

....

....

....

....

....

....

Day 7 Did you feel this week that it would have been advantageous to follow this quote? What were the circumstances?

....

....

....

....

....

....

....

....

....

....

....

....

....

....

....

....

....

....

....

Day 1 What is your initial reaction to this painting?
How does it make you feel?

....

....

....

....

....

....

....

....

....

....

....

....

Day 2 Is there something going on in your life right now or something from the past that makes you relate to this image?

....

....

....

....

....

....

....

....

....

....

....

....

....

....

....

....

....

....

....

Day 3 Who is the person in the painting? Write a brief character description.

....

....

....

....

....

....

....

....

....

....

....

....

....

....

....

....

....

....

....

Day 4 What is the person's mood? What has just happened to them and how are they feeling?

....

....

....

....

....

....

....

....

....

....

....

....

....

....

....

....

....

....

....

....

Day 5 Have you ever felt this way? What were the circumstances?

....

....

....

....

....

....

....

....

....

....

....

....

....

....

....

....

....

....

....

....

....

Day 6 Describe the place/setting. Where is it? What is it?

....

....

....

....

....

....

....

....

....

....

....

....

....

....

....

....

....

....

....

....

Day 7 Do you have a place like this in your life where you can go when you are feeling the same as the character?

....

....

....

....

....

....

....

....

....

....

....

....

....

....

....

....

....

....

....

"I won't think of it now. I can't stand it now. I'll think of it later."

Day 1 When was the last time you felt this way? Why?

....

....

....

....

....

....

....

....

....

....

....

....

....

....

....

....

....

Day 2 Take a moment and create a story around someone who may have said these statements. Write freely for a few minutes.

....
....
....
....
....
....
....
....
....
....
....
....
....
....
....
....
....
....
....
....

Day 3 Look back at yesterday's entry: Do you relate to the character you created? Why or why not?

....
....
....
....
....
....
....
....
....
....
....
....
....
....
....
....
....
....
....
....

Day 4 What happened today that you would rather not think about?

....

....

....

....

....

....

....

....

....

....

....

....

....

....

....

....

....

....

....

....

Day 5 Is there value in thinking of things later? What?

....

....

....

....

....

....

....

....

....

....

....

....

....

....

....

....

....

....

....

....

Day 6 Do you value the idea of not thinking on things? Why or why not?

....
....
....
....
....
....
....
....
....
....
....
....
....
....
....
....
....
....
....
....
....

Day 7 Is this a good way to live?

....

....

....

....

....

....

....

....

....

....

....

....

....

....

....

....

....

....

If repeat characters appear in your writing, it suggests unsettled feelings about these particular relationships.

Day 1 Describe this scene. Is it inviting, lonely, or something else?

....

....

....

....

....

....

....

....

....

....

....

Day 2 When was the last time you sat down and just enjoyed the day?

....
....
....
....
....
....
....
....
....
....
....
....
....
....
....
....
....
....
....
....

Day 3 Have you needed to relax this week yet? If this scene were not your ideal setting, what would be?

....

....

....

....

....

....

....

....

....

....

....

....

....

....

....

....

....

....

....

....

....

Day 4 Who might have taken this picture? Why?

....

....

....

....

....

....

....

....

....

....

....

....

....

....

....

....

....

....

....

....

....

Day 5 Create a story about this photograph. Do you relate to the characters?

....

....

....

....

....

....

....

....

....

....

....

....

....

....

....

....

....

....

....

....

....

Day 6 How could this scene fit into your life today? Is it a positive or negative fit?

....

....

....

....

....

....

....

....

....

....

....

....

....

....

....

....

....

....

....

Day 7 Look back at your response to Day 1 of this week. Has your outlook on the scene changed since then? Why or why not?

....

....

....

....

....

....

....

....

....

....

....

....

....

....

....

....

....

....

....

"I have visited him again and found him sitting in a corner brooding. When I came in he threw himself on his knees before me and implored me to let him have a cat; that his salvation depended upon it. I was firm, however, and told him that he could not have it, whereupon he went without a word, and sat down, gnawing his fingers, in the corner where I had found him."

Day 1 Read the passage. Describe the mood of it. How does it make you feel?

....

....

....

....

....

....

....

....

....

....

....

....

Day 2 Is there something in your life that you feel you cannot do without? What is it? Why?

....

....

....

....

....

....

....

....

....

....

....

....

....

....

....

....

....

....

....

....

....

Day 3 What has someone denied you that you thought you could not do without? How did this make you feel?

....

....

....

....

....

....

....

....

....

....

....

....

....

....

....

....

....

....

....

....

Day 4 Who are the two people in this scene? Describe them and their relationship.

....
....
....
....
....
....
....
....
....
....
....
....
....
....
....
....
....
....
....
....
....

Day 5 Where does this scene take place? Describe it and what may go on there.

....

....

....

....

....

....

....

....

....

....

....

....

....

....

....

....

....

....

....

....

....

Day 6 Do you think there are other people present or nearby our two characters? Who might they be?

....

....

....

....

....

....

....

....

....

....

....

....

....

....

....

....

....

....

....

....

Day 7 Which character do you relate to the most and why?

....
....
....
....
....
....
....
....
....
....
....
....
....
....
....
....
....
....

The way we feel shapes our perception. Notice how your mood in any given week impacted your reaction to the prompts.

Day 1 What would you name this painting? How does it relate to something going on in your life right now?

....

....

....

....

....

....

....

....

....

....

....

Day 2 Which of the four figures do you relate to the most today?

....
....
....
....
....
....
....
....
....
....
....
....
....
....
....
....
....
....
....

Day 3 Create a story about one of the darker figures. What was your motivation for the story you just created?

....

....

....

....

....

....

....

....

....

....

....

....

....

....

....

....

....

....

....

....

Day 4 Do you relate to the two women at all? Do you think they have anything in common with modern day women?

....

....

....

....

....

....

....

....

....

....

....

....

....

....

....

....

....

....

....

....

Day 5 What are the two girls talking about? When you see two women talking in this way, what are your initial reactions?

....
....
....
....
....
....
....
....
....
....
....
....
....
....
....
....
....
....
....

Day 6 How do each of the characters feel? When was the last time you felt like one of these characters?

....
....
....
....
....
....
....
....
....
....
....
....
....
....
....
....
....
....
....

Day 7 Think back on the art this week. Did your feelings change about it as the week progressed? What about this week's art were you able to connect to your daily life?

....
....
....
....
....
....
....
....
....
....
....
....
....
....
....
....
....
....
....

"Love is not love
Which alters when it alteration finds,
Or bends with the remover to remove:
O no! it is an ever-fixed mark
That looks on tempests and is never shaken;
It is the star to every wandering bark,
Whose worth's unknown, although his
height be taken."

Day 1 Which part of the quote do you think is most true about love as you've experienced it?

....

....

....

....

....

....

....

....

....

....

....

Day 2 Do you think that when two people love each other they make changes to please the other person? Is this a bad thing?

....

....

....

....

....

....

....

....

....

....

....

....

....

....

....

....

....

....

....

....

Day 3 Create a character who may have spoken these words. Whom is he or she talking to?

....

....

....

....

....

....

....

....

....

....

....

....

....

....

....

....

....

....

....

Day 4 In your life, does this quote seem more fitting to romantic love or familial love?

....

....

....

....

....

....

....

....

....

....

....

....

....

....

....

....

....

....

....

....

Day 5 Do you find this poem realistic? How in your life has it been true and how has it not been?

....
....
....
....
....
....
....
....
....
....
....
....
....
....
....
....
....
....
....
....
....

Day 6 How would you feel if someone expressed
these sentiments about love with you in mind?

....

....

....

....

....

....

....

....

....

....

....

....

....

....

....

....

....

....

....

....

Day 7 Can love be strong, sturdy, and enduring as the quote suggests? Why or why not?

....
....
....
....
....
....
....
....
....
....
....
....
....
....
....
....
....

Emotional concepts, such as love, can be hard to write about; when something is difficult, this may be a sign that we need to deal with it through written or verbal expression.

Day 1 Which couple in this painting stands out to you the most?

....

....

....

....

....

....

....

....

....

....

Day 2 What type of person would be painting this scene? What was their point of view?

....
....
....
....
....
....
....
....
....
....
....
....
....
....
....
....
....
....
....
....

Day 3 Do you think the painter feels like they are on the outside looking in? Have you felt this way recently? When?

....

....

....

....

....

....

....

....

....

....

....

....

....

....

....

....

....

....

....

Day 4 Focus only on the colors. What do you feel?

....

....

....

....

....

....

....

....

....

....

....

....

....

....

....

....

....

....

....

Day 5 This painting is very defined in some places and blurred in others. Which appeals to you more? Why?

....

....

....

....

....

....

....

....

....

....

....

....

....

....

....

....

....

....

....

....

Day 6 Look at the two young women in the center of the picture. Who are they and what are they talking about?

....
....
....
....
....
....
....
....
....
....
....
....
....
....
....
....
....
....
....

Day 7 There are many different couples in this picture. Choose a pair that stands out to you and create a story about them. Why did you choose that particular couple?

....
....
....
....
....
....
....
....
....
....
....
....
....
....
....
....
....
....
....
....

"They'll grow up with what the psychologists used to call an 'instinctive' hatred of books and flowers. Reflexes unalterably conditioned. They'll be safe from books and botany all their lives."

Day 1 Take three minutes and write whatever comes to mind after reading this passage. What would you call it?

....

....

....

....

....

....

....

....

....

....

....

....

....

....

Day 2 Have you ever felt like you do things without thinking? Did you make choices today that you felt you were not in control of?

....
....
....
....
....
....
....
....
....
....
....
....
....
....
....
....
....
....
....
....

Day 3 Who is the speaker of this passage? Where are they coming from? Do you share their views?

....
....
....
....
....
....
....
....
....
....
....
....
....
....
....
....
....
....
....

Day 4 Does this passage disturb you? Has something disturbed you today? If so, what could you have done differently to change the outcome?

....
....
....
....
....
....
....
....
....
....
....
....
....
....
....
....
....
....

Day 5 What about this passage speaks to you in the context of what you have experienced today?

....
....
....
....
....
....
....
....
....
....
....
....
....
....
....
....
....
....
....
....
....

Day 6 Is this a modern passage? What about it can you relate to?

....
....
....
....
....
....
....
....
....
....
....
....
....
....
....
....
....
....
....
....

Day 7 Often times we make decisions without thinking them through. Did this happen to you this week? When?

....

....

....

....

....

....

....

....

....

....

....

....

....

....

....

....

> *Look for recurrent themes in the free writing exercises, as they may reveal what weighs heavy on your heart and mind.*

Day 1 Take a minute to look at this painting. What kind of mood does it evoke? What would you call it?

....

....

....

....

....

....

....

....

....

....

....

Day 2 Who are the characters? What is their relationship?

....

....

....

....

....

....

....

....

....

....

....

....

....

....

....

....

....

....

....

....

Day 3 Describe a similar relationship you have in your life, or a relationship you wish you had.

....

....

....

....

....

....

....

....

....

....

....

....

....

....

....

....

....

....

....

....

....

Day 4 The young girl appears to be watching something. Describe what she is watching.

....

....

....

....

....

....

....

....

....

....

....

....

....

....

....

....

....

....

....

....

....

Day 5 Tell a short story about why the lady is wearing black.

....

....

....

....

....

....

....

....

....

....

....

....

....

....

....

....

....

....

....

....

....

Day 6 Why are the characters out today? Where are they going or where have they come from?

....
....
....
....
....
....
....
....
....
....
....
....
....
....
....
....
....
....

Day 7 Looking back at this week's answers, do you recognize either of the characters or situations from your own life? Has anything in your life this week influenced your answers or the way you interpreted this painting? How?

....
....
....
....
....
....
....
....
....
....
....
....
....
....
....
....

Sometimes colors bring up emotions. If bright, colorful pictures cause anxiety, it suggests difficulty processing complex feelings.

Quarterly Summary

Day 1 Look back over the past three months. Which was your favorite piece of art? Why?

....

....

....

....

....

....

....

....

....

....

....

....

....

....

....

Day 2 Examine your chosen piece. Why do you like it? What did it teach you about yourself?

....

....

....

....

....

....

....

....

....

....

....

....

....

....

....

....

....

....

....

....

....

Day 3 Think back to three months ago. Would your favorite choice have been the same as now?

....

....

....

....

....

....

....

....

....

....

....

....

....

....

....

....

....

....

....

....

....

Day 4 Look back over the literature you read so far. Which was your favorite piece? Why?

....

....

....

....

....

....

....

....

....

....

....

....

....

....

....

....

....

....

....

....

....

Day 5 What is it about this piece that excites you? Do you think the style of literature influenced your choice? How?

....
....
....
....
....
....
....
....
....
....
....
....
....
....
....
....
....
....
....
....
....

Day 6 Think back to three months ago. Would your favorite choice in literature have been the same as now?

....

....

....

....

....

....

....

....

....

....

....

....

....

....

....

....

....

....

Day 7 Did you have trouble choosing the pieces? Why? Do you think your mood influenced your choices?

....

....

....

....

....

....

....

....

....

....

....

....

....

....

....

As you review your work, look for patterns in your reactions. Patterns in any response in life reveal unconscious issues that are struggling to break through to the surface of consciousness.

Day 1 Look at this photo for a while. Now cover it up and describe the house.

....

....

....

....

....

....

....

....

....

....

....

Day 2 Who lives in this house? Describe them.

....
....
....
....
....
....
....
....
....
....
....
....
....
....
....
....
....
....
....
....

Day 3 What is a typical day like for the people you have described?

....
....
....
....
....
....
....
....
....
....
....
....
....
....
....
....
....
....
....
....
....

Day 4 What do you want the inside of the house to look like?

....

....

....

....

....

....

....

....

....

....

....

....

....

....

....

....

....

....

....

....

Day 5 How do you fit into this house? Is it someplace you would like to live?

....

....

....

....

....

....

....

....

....

....

....

....

....

....

....

....

....

....

....

....

Day 6 Think about this house you have described and where you live now. Which do you prefer and why?

....

....

....

....

....

....

....

....

....

....

....

....

....

....

....

....

....

....

....

....

Day 7 Take some time to think about your "dream" house and then describe it. How can you achieve this dream?

....

....

....

....

....

....

....

....

....

....

....

....

....

....

....

....

....

....

....

"'Maybe... you'll fall in love with me all over again. Hell,' I said, 'I love you enough now. What do you want to do? Ruin me?' 'Yes. I want to ruin you.' 'Good,' I said, 'That's what I want too.'"

Day 1 What is your initial reaction to this dialogue?

....

....

....

....

....

....

....

....

....

....

....

....

....

....

Day 2 Have you ever felt that love has the potential to cause ruin? When? With whom?

....
....
....
....
....
....
....
....
....
....
....
....
....
....
....
....
....
....
....
....
....
....

Day 3 Why is it brave to accept love? What do you have to lose by accepting love?

....

....

....

....

....

....

....

....

....

....

....

....

....

....

....

....

....

....

....

....

....

Day 4 Is there strength in accepting love? Why or why not?

....
....
....
....
....
....
....
....
....
....
....
....
....
....
....
....
....
....
....
....
....

Day 5 This statement correlates love and destruction. Do you think these two concepts belong together?

....

....

....

....

....

....

....

....

....

....

....

....

....

....

....

....

....

....

....

....

....

Day 6 Could this passage have fit into your life recently? If so, how?

....
....
....
....
....
....
....
....
....
....
....
....
....
....
....
....
....
....
....
....
....

Day 7 The word "enough" is peculiar in this statement. Do people have to earn love, or do we deserve it?

....
....
....
....
....
....
....
....
....
....
....
....
....
....
....
....
....
....
....
....

Day 1 What is your first impression of this painting? What would you call it?

....

....

....

....

....

....

....

....

....

....

....

Day 2 Who is this girl? Write a character description of her.

....

....

....

....

....

....

....

....

....

....

....

....

....

....

....

....

....

....

....

....

....

Day 3 What do you think her family is like? How is
it similar or different from yours?

....
....
....
....
....
....
....
....
....
....
....
....
....
....
....
....
....
....
....
....
....

Day 4 Based on her expression and your description of her, write an article for the paper she is reading.

....
....
....
....
....
....
....
....
....
....
....
....
....
....
....
....
....
....
....
....

Day 5 How does she react to this news? What news could you read that would make you react in a similar way?

....
....
....
....
....
....
....
....
....
....
....
....
....
....
....
....
....
....
....

Day 6 Where do you think she is right now, reading this news? Why is she there?

....
....
....
....
....
....
....
....
....
....
....
....
....
....
....
....
....
....
....

Day 7 Looking back on the little stories you have created for this painting, how does your current impression compare to your first impression? How did imagining this different world every day affect your thoughts?

....
....
....
....
....
....
....
....
....
....
....
....
....
....
....
....
....
....
....
....

"She felt that she could so much more depend upon the sincerity of those who sometimes looked or said a careless or hasty thing, than of those whose presence of mind never varied, whose tongue never slipped."

Day 1 Is this statement optimistic or pessimistic? Why?

....

....

....

....

....

....

....

....

....

....

....

....

....

....

....

Day 2 What kind of person is "she"? Why do you think she feels this way?

....
....
....
....
....
....
....
....
....
....
....
....
....
....
....
....
....
....
....
....
....

Day 3 Is it the beginning of the story or the end?
Write a short story that starts with or finishes with the
statement.

....

....

....

....

....

....

....

....

....

....

....

....

....

....

....

....

....

....

....

Day 4 Who are the characters in your story? Do you recognize them from your life?

....
....
....
....
....
....
....
....
....
....
....
....
....
....
....
....
....
....
....
....

Day 5 Can you relate to "she"? Describe an experience in your life where you felt this way.

....

....

....

....

....

....

....

....

....

....

....

....

....

....

....

....

....

....

Day 6 Describe someone in your life whose "mind never varied..." Do you trust them? Would you take advice from them?

....
....
....
....
....
....
....
....
....
....
....
....
....
....
....
....
....
....
....
....
....

Day 7 Think about this statement. Has your opinion of it changed? Do you think there is truth in it? Why or why not?

....

....

....

....

....

....

....

....

....

....

....

....

....

....

....

....

....

Pay attention to your reaction to female characters and narrators versus male. Your feelings towards the different genders likely reflect how you respond in daily life.

Month Five

Day 1 What is your initial reaction to this picture? Take 2 minutes and write the first thoughts and feelings that come into your head.

....

....

....

....

....

....

....

....

....

....

Day 2 Where do you imagine this takes place? Did you see anything in your life today that reminded you of this scene?

....
....
....
....
....
....
....
....
....
....
....
....
....
....
....
....
....
....
....
....

Day 3 Who is the person in the picture? Write a story about what he or she is doing.

....
....
....
....
....
....
....
....
....
....
....
....
....
....
....
....
....
....
....

Day 4 Pretend you are one of the butterflies. How do you feel? What are you thinking? Did you feel that way at all today?

....

....

....

....

....

....

....

....

....

....

....

....

....

....

....

....

....

....

....

....

Day 5 Is this a pleasant painting or does it disturb you? Why?

....

....

....

....

....

....

....

....

....

....

....

....

....

....

....

....

....

....

....

....

Day 6 Create a story about the shadow in the front of the picture. What or who is it? How do you think your day will shape your thoughts and feelings about it?

....

....

....

....

....

....

....

....

....

....

....

....

....

....

....

....

....

....

....

....

Day 7 Think back over the past week. Did your
opinions change about the painting?

....

....

....

....

....

....

....

....

....

....

....

....

....

....

....

....

....

....

....

....

*"There is a sort of pleasing half-guilty blush,
where the blood is more in fault than the man;
'tis sent impetuous from the heart, and virtue
flies after it, – not to call it back, but to make
the sensation of it more delicious to the nerves; –
'tis associated."*

Day 1 Has there been a time recently when you
blushed? When? Why?

....
....
....
....
....
....
....
....
....
....
....
....
....
....

Day 2 When has your body controlled your reactions more than your mind? What were the circumstances?

....

....

....

....

....

....

....

....

....

....

....

....

....

....

....

....

....

....

....

....

Day 3 Who said this? How can you relate to the author?

....
....
....
....
....
....
....
....
....
....
....
....
....
....
....
....
....
....
....
....
....

Day 4 When this week has your heart overpowered your mind?

....
....
....
....
....
....
....
....
....
....
....
....
....
....
....
....
....
....
....
....
....

Day 5 This quote is quite emotional. How do you think your day shaped your thoughts and feelings about it?

....
....
....
....
....
....
....
....
....
....
....
....
....
....
....
....
....
....
....
....

Day 6 Is there anything appealing about being on edge or nervous? When was the last time you felt this way?

....
....
....
....
....
....
....
....
....
....
....
....
....
....
....
....
....
....
....

Day 7 What does the author mean when they say that the blood is more at fault than the man? When this week have your felt out of control of your bodily reactions?

....

....

....

....

....

....

....

....

....

....

....

....

....

....

....

....

....

....

....

Day 1 What is your first impression of this painting? What would you call it?

....

....

....

....

....

....

....

....

....

....

....

Day 2 Where do you think this is? Describe the place.

....

....

....

....

....

....

....

....

....

....

....

....

....

....

....

....

....

....

....

....

Day 3 Describe the characters in the painting. Who are they? Are they related?

....

....

....

....

....

....

....

....

....

....

....

....

....

....

....

....

....

....

....

....

....

Day 4 Describe what is beyond or in the trees in the center of the painting.

....

....

....

....

....

....

....

....

....

....

....

....

....

....

....

....

....

....

....

....

....

Day 5 Write a story about the characters and place you created.

....

....

....

....

....

....

....

....

....

....

....

....

....

....

....

....

....

....

....

....

....

Day 6 How do you fit into the story? Is it someplace you would like to visit or live?

....
....
....
....
....
....
....
....
....
....
....
....
....
....
....
....
....
....
....
....

Day 7 How did looking back and imagining this painting affect your mood this week? Did you look forward to it or dread it? Why?

....

....

....

....

....

....

....

....

....

....

....

....

....

....

....

....

If you have an easier time engaging with landscapes than character pictures, you may be more of an introvert who finds peace in solitude. Extroverts tend to find relaxation with others.

"I wanted to live deep and suck out all the marrow of life… to drive life into a corner, and reduce it to its lowest terms, and, if it proved to be mean, why then to get the whole and genuine meanness of it, publish its meanness to the world; or if it were sublime to know it by experience, and be able to give a true account of it in my next excursion."

Day 1 What is your initial reaction to these statements? Do any of the words stand out to you in particular? Why?

....

....

....

....

....

....

....

....

....

....

....

Day 2 What does the "meanness" invoke in you?
Have you felt this word in any context this week?

....

....

....

....

....

....

....

....

....

....

....

....

....

....

....

....

....

....

....

....

Day 3 Is this quote positive or negative? Why? How do you think your day influenced your answer?

....

....

....

....

....

....

....

....

....

....

....

....

....

....

....

....

....

....

....

....

Day 4 Who could have said this? Make up a short past for that person. Do you relate?

....
....
....
....
....
....
....
....
....
....
....
....
....
....
....
....
....
....
....
....
....
....

Day 5 What does the author mean by "living deep"? Have you felt this way recently?

....

....

....

....

....

....

....

....

....

....

....

....

....

....

....

....

....

....

....

....

Day 6 Describe one event in your life where these statements have proven true.

....

....

....

....

....

....

....

....

....

....

....

....

....

....

....

....

....

....

....

....

....

Day 7 Look back at your initial reaction to this statement. Has it changed based on your week? Why or why not?

....
....
....
....
....
....
....
....
....
....
....
....
....
....
....
....
....
....
....

Day 1 What are your first impressions of this path? Why?

....

....

....

....

....

....

....

....

....

....

....

Day 2 Is this path daunting or welcoming? What in your life has seemed either daunting or welcoming this week?

....
....
....
....
....
....
....
....
....
....
....
....
....
....
....
....
....
....
....
....
....

Day 3 What new paths have you created this week?

....
....
....
....
....
....
....
....
....
....
....
....
....
....
....
....
....
....
....
....

Day 4 Is this path narrow or wide? Has your life felt narrow or wide this week in any way?

....

....

....

....

....

....

....

....

....

....

....

....

....

....

....

....

....

....

....

....

Day 5 An interesting facet of this path is that it has stones to follow. Is that comforting to you, or do you prefer to find your own way?

....

....

....

....

....

....

....

....

....

....

....

....

....

....

....

....

....

....

....

....

Day 6 Who do you think built this particular path in this alley? Why?

....
....
....
....
....
....
....
....
....
....
....
....
....
....
....
....
....
....
....

Day 7 Look back at your response to Day 6. Sometimes in life we have to create off-beat paths to get to where we need to go. Has this happened to you recently? When and how?

....
....
....
....
....
....
....
....
....
....
....
....
....
....
....
....
....
....
....

"I have frequently detected myself in such kind of mistakes... in a total misapprehension of character at some point or other: fancying people so much more gay or grave, or ingenious or stupid than they really are and I can hardly tell why, or in what the deception originated."

Day 1 Read this passage through a couple of times. What are your initial thoughts about it?

....

....

....

....

....

....

....

....

....

....

....

....

....

Day 2 Who is the speaker of this passage? Describe their mood.

....

....

....

....

....

....

....

....

....

....

....

....

....

....

....

....

....

....

....

....

....

Day 3 Tell the speaker's story. What action or event led him or her to say these things?

....

....

....

....

....

....

....

....

....

....

....

....

....

....

....

....

....

....

....

Day 4 Does the speaker appear upset about the mistake he or she has made? According to your story, how does this all work out? Good, bad, ugly?

....

....

....

....

....

....

....

....

....

....

....

....

....

....

....

....

....

....

....

....

Day 5 The speaker talks about misjudging people's character. Have you ever found yourself doing this? What was the situation?

....

....

....

....

....

....

....

....

....

....

....

....

....

....

....

....

....

....

....

Day 6 Speaking to your answer on Day 5, were you disappointed in your "misapprehension"? How did it affect your relationship with the person?

....

....

....

....

....

....

....

....

....

....

....

....

....

....

....

....

....

....

....

....

....

Day 7 Write about a time when you misjudged someone's character and were pleasantly surprised. How did your realization improve your relationship?

....

....

....

....

....

....

....

....

....

....

....

....

....

....

....

....

> *Difficult passages can be either intriguing or frustrating. Notice if your mood or week impacts whether or not you like the more difficult quotes. This reflects how stress changes your ability to manage the complex problems of life.*

Day 1 Whom do you identify at the top of this picture? Why?

....

....

....

....

....

....

....

....

....

....

....

Day 2 Look at the woman at the bottom of the page. What is she feeling? Can you relate?

....

....

....

....

....

....

....

....

....

....

....

....

....

....

....

....

....

....

....

....

Day 3 Examine the couples in this picture. Do they seem happy? Why or why not?

....
....
....
....
....
....
....
....
....
....
....
....
....
....
....
....
....
....
....
....
....

Day 4 Does the overall imagery of this picture make you uncomfortable?

....

....

....

....

....

....

....

....

....

....

....

....

....

....

....

....

....

....

....

....

Day 5 If you look at this picture and feel contentment, why do you think this is so?

....
....
....
....
....
....
....
....
....
....
....
....
....
....
....
....
....
....
....
....
....

Day 6 Do you wish there was color in this picture?

....
....
....
....
....
....
....
....
....
....
....
....
....
....
....
....
....
....
....
....
....

Day 7 Take a few moments to reflect on this painting. What is the first thing that comes to mind?

....

....

....

....

....

....

....

....

....

....

....

....

....

....

....

....

....

....

....

....

Quarterly Summary

Day 1 As you read through your art entries, are you surprised? Do you notice any change from month to month? What is it that has changed?

....

....

....

....

....

....

....

....

....

....

....

....

....

....

....

Day 2 As you read through your literature entries, are you surprised at what you read? Are you in the same place now?

....
....
....
....
....
....
....
....
....
....
....
....
....
....
....
....
....
....
....
....

Day 3 As you read through some of the stories you have written, how do you feel you have progressed as a story teller? Did it get easier or harder with each piece?

....
....
....
....
....
....
....
....
....
....
....
....
....
....
....
....
....
....
....

Day 4 One of the first literature passages talks about storing the mind. Do you feel you have stored your mind with more positive thoughts over the year? How has writing and imagining different situations helped you from day to day?

....
....
....
....
....
....
....
....
....
....
....
....
....
....
....
....
....
....
....

Day 5 Some of the prompts asked you to describe or invent worlds and people that were not shown in the piece. What did you like and dislike about this exercise? Did it get easier?

....
....
....
....
....
....
....
....
....
....
....
....
....
....
....
....
....
....
....

Day 6 Recognizing that there was a pattern in the exercises and a touch of repetition, what did you find yourself looking forward to the most? How did that particular exercise make you feel?

....

....

....

....

....

....

....

....

....

....

....

....

....

....

....

....

....

....

....

Day 7 What exercises did you dread? How did it make you feel when you would come upon one? What could you do to change that feeling?

....

....

....

....

....

....

....

....

....

....

....

....

....

....

....

....

....

....

....

Month Seven

Day 1 Take a moment to take in this painting. What mood does it evoke? What would you call it?

....

....

....

....

....

....

....

....

....

....

Day 2 Who is this man? Where does he come from? Where does he fit socially and economically?

....

....

....

....

....

....

....

....

....

....

....

....

....

....

....

....

....

....

....

....

....

Day 3 Can you relate to the character you just described? How is he like you?

....

....

....

....

....

....

....

....

....

....

....

....

....

....

....

....

....

....

....

....

Day 4 Tell a story about what has happened to him right before this picture was painted. Explain why he holds the expression he does.

....

....

....

....

....

....

....

....

....

....

....

....

....

....

....

....

....

....

....

....

Day 5 What could happen in your life that would give you the same expression or reaction?

....
....
....
....
....
....
....
....
....
....
....
....
....
....
....
....
....
....
....
....

Day 6 The background of the painting is very muddy and vague. Study it for a minute and describe in detail the room or place in which the man stands.

....

....

....

....

....

....

....

....

....

....

....

....

....

....

....

....

....

....

....

....

Day 7 After studying the painting this week, have your initial ideas about it changed? Would you call it something different?

....
....
....
....
....
....
....
....
....
....
....
....
....
....
....
....
....
....
....

"This trait of kindness moved me sensibly."

Day 1 Who might have said this? Under what circumstances?

....

....

....

....

....

....

....

....

....

....

....

....

....

....

....

....

....

Day 2 Have you ever had a situation where you could have truthfully made this statement? When?

....
....
....
....
....
....
....
....
....
....
....
....
....
....
....
....
....
....
....
....

Day 3 When was the last time you did something that may have caused someone to say this about you?

....
....
....
....
....
....
....
....
....
....
....
....
....
....
....
....
....
....
....
....
....

Day 4 Does kindness still move people in our world? How?

....

....

....

....

....

....

....

....

....

....

....

....

....

....

....

....

....

....

....

....

Day 5 When have you needed this statement to be true this week?

....
....
....
....
....
....
....
....
....
....
....
....
....
....
....
....
....
....
....

Day 6 Create a short story around this statement.
Once you've finished, take a moment to observe the
story you created. Was it a romance? A friendship?

....
....
....
....
....
....
....
....
....
....
....
....
....
....
....
....
....
....
....
....

Day 7 Go back to Day 6's prompt. How do you relate to your story?

....
....
....
....
....
....
....
....
....
....
....
....
....
....
....
....
....
....

Short statements are often rich despite their size. If you react to the smaller passages more than the broader quotes, it may mean you see the details of a situation over the bigger picture.

Day 1 Take a few minutes to look at this painting. Be sure to really look in all the corners and dark places. Jot down a few of the main events. Now give it a title.

....

....

....

....

....

....

....

....

....

....

....

Day 2 Pick one of the characters and tell a story about what is happening from their perspective.

....

....

....

....

....

....

....

....

....

....

....

....

....

....

....

....

....

....

....

....

....

Day 3 Now pick someone else and tell the same story from their perspective.

....
....
....
....
....
....
....
....
....
....
....
....
....
....
....
....
....
....
....
....
....

Day 4 The characters in the painting seem to be paired up. Pick a pair and write out the dialog they might be having in the scene.

....

....

....

....

....

....

....

....

....

....

....

....

....

....

....

....

....

....

....

Day 5 Look at the painting again and review your answers from Day 1. Now describe what you see and what you think is going on as an outsider.

....
....
....
....
....
....
....
....
....
....
....
....
....
....
....
....
....
....
....
....

Day 6 Look back on your stories over the last couple of days. Notice the three different perspectives of the same scene. Describe a situation in your life where you feel there were different perspectives of the same event.

....
....
....
....
....
....
....
....
....
....
....
....
....
....
....
....
....
....
....

Day 7 Think about this week's exercises. Taking what you have learned about perspective, how can you use this in your life to change the way you view a situation? Do you think looking at it from different angles is helpful? What is your "perspective"?

....

....

....

....

....

....

....

....

....

....

....

....

....

....

....

....

....

....

....

"I love to rise in a summer morn
When the birds sing on every tree;
The distant huntsman winds his horn,
And the skylark sings with me.
Oh, what sweet company!"

Day 1 What is your initial reaction to this passage? I
you could give this a name, what would it be?

....

....

....

....

....

....

....

....

....

....

....

....

....

....

Day 2 Can you imagine yourself in this scene? Did you feel this way when you woke up this morning?

....

....

....

....

....

....

....

....

....

....

....

....

....

....

....

....

....

....

....

....

Day 3 What feelings are evoked today when you read this passage? Is it too idealistic for you at this point in life?

....

....

....

....

....

....

....

....

....

....

....

....

....

....

....

....

....

....

....

....

Day 4 What would need to happen in your life for your mornings to resemble this passage? Would you want your life that way?

....
....
....
....
....
....
....
....
....
....
....
....
....
....
....
....
....
....
....
....

Day 5 Create a character to narrate this passage. What from your week shaped your response?

....
....
....
....
....
....
....
....
....
....
....
....
....
....
....
....
....
....
....
....

Day 6 Complete the sentence: When I woke up this morning _____. How does your experience compare with the passage?

....
....
....
....
....
....
....
....
....
....
....
....
....
....
....
....
....
....
....
....

Day 7 Think back on the passage for this week. What feelings do you have about it now? Are they different from how you felt on Day 1? Did this passage have any meaning for you in your daily life this week?

....

....

....

....

....

....

....

....

....

....

....

....

....

....

....

....

....

....

Month Eight

Day 1 Look at the painting for a few minutes. What
is the mood? What would you call it?

....

....

....

....

....

....

....

....

....

....

Day 2 All three have distinctively different looks about them. Describe what each one is thinking or feeling.

....
....
....
....
....
....
....
....
....
....
....
....
....
....
....
....
....
....
....
....

Day 3 Of the three, whom do you relate to the most? Why?

....
....
....
....
....
....
....
....
....
....
....
....
....
....
....
....
....
....
....
....
....

Day 4 What circumstance has brought these people here? Where are they headed?

....

....

....

....

....

....

....

....

....

....

....

....

....

....

....

....

....

....

....

Day 5 Way in the background there is a house. Who lives there? Tell a story about someone who lives there.

....

....

....

....

....

....

....

....

....

....

....

....

....

....

....

....

....

....

....

....

....

Day 6 Looking back at what you have written about the characters, do they resemble people you know today? Who? And do you like these people?

....
....
....
....
....
....
....
....
....
....
....
....
....
....
....
....
....
....
....
....
....

Day 7 Compare this setting to where and how you
live today. What are the things that are appealing?
How could you make your life today more like this?

....
....
....
....
....
....
....
....
....
....
....
....
....
....
....
....

Strong reactions to relationship-focused pictures and passages
suggest the need to change patterns of interaction with others.
Take a moment to reflect on how these prompts have affected
the way you view interpersonal relationships in your life.

"The mind is its own place, and in itself can make a heaven of hell and a hell of heaven."

Day 1 What are your first thoughts after reading this statement?

....
....
....
....
....
....
....
....
....
....
....
....
....
....
....
....

Day 2 Is the mind a place of its own? What exterior influences does your mind have on a daily basis?

....

....

....

....

....

....

....

....

....

....

....

....

....

....

....

....

....

....

....

....

Day 3 Does the mind have power? What has happened in your week so far to make this true or not?

....

....

....

....

....

....

....

....

....

....

....

....

....

....

....

....

....

....

....

....

Day 4 Can our mind influence our surroundings?
Has this happened to you this week?

....
....
....
....
....
....
....
....
....
....
....
....
....
....
....
....
....
....
....
....
....

Day 5 Do you think your thoughts drive you to change things in your life?

....
....
....
....
....
....
....
....
....
....
....
....
....
....
....
....
....
....
....
....
....

Day 6 Who could have written this statement? Do you relate to his or her frame of mind?

....

....

....

....

....

....

....

....

....

....

....

....

....

....

....

....

....

....

....

....

....

Day 7 Can you think of a time when your own thoughts made something better or worse? When? What were the circumstances?

....

....

....

....

....

....

....

....

....

....

....

....

....

....

....

....

....

....

....

....

Day 1 Give the city in this painting a name and write about its history and people.

....
....
....
....
....
....
....
....
....
....
....

Day 2 Put yourself in the city you just created. What is your story in this setting?

....

....

....

....

....

....

....

....

....

....

....

....

....

....

....

....

....

....

....

....

Day 3 Who are the people in the foreground? What are they doing?

....

....

....

....

....

....

....

....

....

....

....

....

....

....

....

....

....

....

....

....

....

Day 4 The people you have described, are these people you would like to know? Do they remind you of someone in your life now? Who and why?

....

....

....

....

....

....

....

....

....

....

....

....

....

....

....

....

....

....

....

....

Day 5 Would you like to live in a place like this? What about it appeals or does not appeal to you?

....
....
....
....
....
....
....
....
....
....
....
....
....
....
....
....
....
....
....
....
....

Day 6 Compare the city you have created with the city you live in. Which do you prefer? Would you change anything about where you live? What and why?

....

....

....

....

....

....

....

....

....

....

....

....

....

....

....

....

....

....

Day 7 Look back at the painting and your descriptions. What does this painting make you think about now? How has this changed from the beginning of the week?

....
....
....
....
....
....
....
....
....
....
....
....
....
....
....
....
....
....
....

"I had taken up my binoculars... The woods were unmoved, like a mask—heavy, like the closed door of a prison—they looked with their air of hidden knowledge, of patient expectation, of unapproachable silence."

Day 1 What is your initial reaction to this passage? What would you name it?

....

....

....

....

....

....

....

....

....

....

....

....

Day 2 Where do you think this takes place? If you were suddenly dropped into this world, how would you feel?

....
....
....
....
....
....
....
....
....
....
....
....
....
....
....
....
....
....
....
....

Day 3 Do you think it feels like something unexpected is about to happen in this scene? How do you feel when something unexpected happens to you?

....

....

....

....

....

....

....

....

....

....

....

....

....

....

....

....

....

....

....

Day 4 How do you think the narrator feels? So far this week, have you felt the same way?

....
....
....
....
....
....
....
....
....
....
....
....
....
....
....
....
....
....
....

Day 5 Write a story about the author. Who is he or she? Would you want to be friends with the person you've created?

....

....

....

....

....

....

....

....

....

....

....

....

....

....

....

....

....

....

....

Day 6 Is this passage dark or hopeful? Does it mirror how you've felt today in any way?

....
....
....
....
....
....
....
....
....
....
....
....
....
....
....
....
....
....
....

Day 7 Think back over your week and complete the following sentence in light of the kind of week you've had: This passage makes me think_____.

....
....
....
....
....
....
....
....
....
....
....
....
....
....
....

The prompts are becoming more emotionally salient as the year progresses. The journal process may be less comfortable at times, but this means personal growth is happening!

Month Nine

Day 1 What is your first impression of this painting? What would you call it?

....
....
....
....
....
....
....
....
....
....

Day 2 Who are the man and woman? Give them names. Where are they going and why?

....

....

....

....

....

....

....

....

....

....

....

....

....

....

....

....

....

....

....

....

Day 3 If you could go anywhere, where would you go? Whom would you go with?

....

....

....

....

....

....

....

....

....

....

....

....

....

....

....

....

....

....

....

....

Day 4 What do you think these two are leaving behind? How do they feel about that?

....
....
....
....
....
....
....
....
....
....
....
....
....
....
....
....
....
....
....

Day 5 What in your life would be hard for you to leave behind? What does it mean to you? Why would you miss it?

....

....

....

....

....

....

....

....

....

....

....

....

....

....

....

....

....

....

....

Day 6 Look at the couple again. Do they look excited about their journey? Describe a time in your life when you felt nervous about where you were headed. How did it turn out?

....

....

....

....

....

....

....

....

....

....

....

....

....

....

....

....

....

....

Day 7 If you could start over, would you? What would you hope to change by doing so? What would you look forward to?

....
....
....
....
....
....
....
....
....
....
....
....
....
....
....
....

Storms on the inside often mirror the external environment. As you write, pay attention to how the world around you influences emotional changes within.

"Heaven knows we need never be ashamed of our tears, for they are rain upon the blinding dust of earth, overlying our hard hearts. I was better after I had cried, than before— more sorry, more aware of my own ingratitude, more gentle."

Day 1 When was the last time you cried? Why?

....
....
....
....
....
....
....
....
....
....
....
....
....
....

Day 2 Do you agree that we should not be ashamed of our tears?

....

....

....

....

....

....

....

....

....

....

....

....

....

....

....

....

....

....

....

....

....

Day 3 Are you better after you've cried? Why or why not?

....
....
....
....
....
....
....
....
....
....
....
....
....
....
....
....
....
....
....

Day 4 Think of a difficult situation you've encountered this week. Would tears have made it better?

....

....

....

....

....

....

....

....

....

....

....

....

....

....

....

....

....

....

....

....

Day 5 Do you hold in your tears? When and why?

....
....
....
....
....
....
....
....
....
....
....
....
....
....
....
....
....
....
....
....
....

Day 6 Why do tears make you more aware of ingratitude?

....
....
....
....
....
....
....
....
....
....
....
....
....
....
....
....
....
....
....
....
....

Day 7 What was the frame of mind of the person who wrote this? Can you relate?

....

....

....

....

....

....

....

....

....

....

....

....

....

....

....

....

....

....

....

....

....

Day 1 Write for one minute the initial feelings and thoughts that surface when you look at this picture.

....

....

....

....

....

....

....

....

....

....

....

Day 2 This landscape is somewhat wild, with quite a few different elements. Do you ever feel this way?

....

....

....

....

....

....

....

....

....

....

....

....

....

....

....

....

....

....

....

....

Day 3 Which place in this picture would you rather spend time, the mountains or the foothills? Why?

....

....

....

....

....

....

....

....

....

....

....

....

....

....

....

....

....

....

....

Day 4 There is clearly a storm brewing in the distance. Is there a storm threatening any area of your life right now?

....
....
....
....
....
....
....
....
....
....
....
....
....
....
....
....
....
....
....
....

Day 5 Write a story about this photographer. Why did he or she want to capture this moment? Can you relate?

....
....
....
....
....
....
....
....
....
....
....
....
....
....
....
....
....
....
....
....

Day 6 Is this image inviting or foreboding? Why?

....

....

....

....

....

....

....

....

....

....

....

....

....

....

....

....

....

....

....

Day 7 Is there hope here? When this week have you felt hope in an unlikely place?

....

....

....

....

....

....

....

....

....

....

....

....

....

....

....

....

....

....

....

....

....

Quarterly Summary

Day 1 Look back over the past three months and choose a piece of art that disturbed you. Why did you choose this particular piece?

....

....

....

....

....

....

....

....

....

....

....

....

....

....

Day 2 Looking at your chosen piece, describe the colors, textures, and composition. What is it about these things that disturb you?

....

....

....

....

....

....

....

....

....

....

....

....

....

....

....

....

....

....

....

....

....

Day 3 Re-read the story you wrote about this piece of art the first time you saw it. Do you still relate to it? How has your outlook changed?

....

....

....

....

....

....

....

....

....

....

....

....

....

....

....

....

....

....

....

Day 4 Look back over the past three months and choose a piece of literature that you did not like or could not relate to. Why did you choose this piece? Has your point of view changed?

....
....
....
....
....
....
....
....
....
....
....
....
....
....
....
....
....
....
....

Day 5 What kind of composition is the piece you chose yesterday? Is it a description or a conversation? Do you think these factors influenced your choice?

....

....

....

....

....

....

....

....

....

....

....

....

....

....

....

....

....

....

....

Day 6 Re-read your entries for this piece. Do you still relate to what you were thinking then? How have you changed?

....

....

....

....

....

....

....

....

....

....

....

....

....

....

....

....

....

....

....

....

Day 7 What has happened to you this week to influence your choices? Do you think your choices would have been the same three months ago?

....
....
....
....
....
....
....
....
....
....
....
....
....
....
....
....
....
....
....

Day 1 What would you title this painting? Why?

....

....

....

....

....

....

....

....

....

....

....

Day 2 What is the mood of these women? Have you felt the same way recently?

....

....

....

....

....

....

....

....

....

....

....

....

....

....

....

....

....

....

....

....

Day 3 What is the relationship between the two characters? Do you have a relationship like this in your life right now?

....

....

....

....

....

....

....

....

....

....

....

....

....

....

....

....

....

....

....

Day 4 Create a story about these two people. Which one do you relate to?

....
....
....
....
....
....
....
....
....
....
....
....
....
....
....
....
....
....
....
....

Day 5 Think about the relationship between these two women. Do you have any relationships like this? How have these relationships impacted your life this week?

....
....
....
....
....
....
....
....
....
....
....
....
....
....
....
....
....
....
....

Day 6 Look at this painting. How does it make you feel? Are the colors comforting or disturbing?

....

....

....

....

....

....

....

....

....

....

....

....

....

....

....

....

....

....

....

....

Day 7 Think about the mood of this painting. Were you able to relate to it this past week?

....
....
....
....
....
....
....
....
....
....
....
....
....
....
....
....
....

Images that blur the lines of reality challenge perception. If you are comfortable with distorted reality, it may suggest a certain level of irreverence in life.

"Gather the fleet flower of your youth,
Take ye your pleasure at the best;
Be merry ere our beauty flit,
For length of days will tarnish it
Like roses that were loveliest."

Day 1 What are your first thoughts about this passage? How would you describe it?

....

....

....

....

....

....

....

....

....

....

....

....

....

....

Day 2 Do you agree or disagree with the advice given? How can you apply it to the way you live your life?

....
....
....
....
....
....
....
....
....
....
....
....
....
....
....
....
....
....
....
....

Day 3 Who is the speaker in this passage? Describe what kind of person he or she is.

....

....

....

....

....

....

....

....

....

....

....

....

....

....

....

....

....

....

....

....

....

Day 4 Who is the listener? Describe the character.

....
....
....
....
....
....
....
....
....
....
....
....
....
....
....
....
....
....
....
....
....

Day 5 Create a story about how these two characters came into this conversation. How do they know each other? What is the conversation about?

....

....

....

....

....

....

....

....

....

....

....

....

....

....

....

....

....

....

....

....

Day 6 Of the two characters you have created, whom do you relate to the most and why?

....
....
....
....
....
....
....
....
....
....
....
....
....
....
....
....
....
....
....
....

Day 7 If you could give advice to anyone, what would you say?

....
....
....
....
....
....
....
....
....
....
....
....
....
....
....
....
....
....
....
....
....

Day 1 Take a few minutes to look at this painting.
Now describe the mood.

....
....
....
....
....
....
....
....
....
....
....

Day 2 Who are these people? Tell a little about each one.

....

....

....

....

....

....

....

....

....

....

....

....

....

....

....

....

....

....

....

Day 3 Are all of the characters equal in this story? Is one in charge? Is one being persecuted? Describe their relationship.

....
....
....
....
....
....
....
....
....
....
....
....
....
....
....
....
....
....
....
....

Day 4 What do you think these three people are talking about? Write out what you imagine their conversation to be.

....
....
....
....
....
....
....
....
....
....
....
....
....
....
....
....
....
....
....
....
....

Day 5 Based on these characters you have described and the circumstance you created, which one do you relate to the most and why?

....
....
....
....
....
....
....
....
....
....
....
....
....
....
....
....
....
....
....
....

Day 6 Do you sometimes wish you felt more like one of the other characters instead? What makes you feel that way?

....
....
....
....
....
....
....
....
....
....
....
....
....
....
....
....
....
....

Day 7 Are there any relationships in your life right now that are like those you have described in this painting? How do they make you feel? What would you change in the relationship to make it better?

....
....
....
....
....
....
....
....
....
....
....
....
....
....
....
....
....
....
....

"In transports of this kind, the heart, in spite of the understanding, will always say too much."

Day 1 When has your heart said too much?

....

....

....

....

....

....

....

....

....

....

....

....

....

....

....

....

Day 2 Has there been a time recently when you felt that you had a keen understanding of a difficult situation?

....

....

....

....

....

....

....

....

....

....

....

....

....

....

....

....

....

....

....

....

Day 3 Create a situation for this quote. What would it be? Why?

....
....
....
....
....
....
....
....
....
....
....
....
....
....
....
....
....
....
....
....

Day 4 Has there been a time this week when despite understanding a situation, you said things you should not have?

....
....
....
....
....
....
....
....
....
....
....
....
....
....
....
....
....
....
....
....
....

Day 5 Who would have said this? Why?

....

....

....

....

....

....

....

....

....

....

....

....

....

....

....

....

....

....

....

Day 6 Is saying too much a bad thing? When and why?

....
....
....
....
....
....
....
....
....
....
....
....
....
....
....
....
....
....
....
....
....

Day 7 When has your heart recently led your speech

....

....

....

....

....

....

....

....

....

....

....

....

....

....

....

....

....

....

In life, the tendency to say too much has a time and place. Reflect on times when saying too much has been positive and when it has not worked out so well. Can you tell the difference?

Day 1 Take a minute to really look at this painting.
What sticks out the most to you? Why?

....
....
....
....
....
....
....
....
....
....
....

Day 2 There is a large basket hanging on the wall in the back. What are its contents? Whom do they belong to?

....

....

....

....

....

....

....

....

....

....

....

....

....

....

....

....

....

....

....

Day 3 Who is the woman in the painting? Write a story about her life.

....
....
....
....
....
....
....
....
....
....
....
....
....
....
....
....
....
....
....

Day 4 What is she making? Whom is she making it for? How does she feel about this chore?

....

....

....

....

....

....

....

....

....

....

....

....

....

....

....

....

....

....

....

Day 5 What is she thinking right now? Write out her inner dialogue. What is the conversation she is having with herself right now?

....
....
....
....
....
....
....
....
....
....
....
....
....
....
....
....
....
....
....
....

Day 6 How do you relate to this woman you have described? Is she someone you know in your life now?

....
....
....
....
....
....
....
....
....
....
....
....
....
....
....
....
....
....

Day 7 If you could, how would you change this painting? What would you do differently to make it more appealing to you? Can you apply any of this to your life?

....

....

....

....

....

....

....

....

....

....

....

....

....

....

....

....

....

....

....

"When people will not weed their own mind, they are apt to be overrun with nettles."

Day 1 What does it mean to "weed" a mind?

....
....
....
....
....
....
....
....
....
....
....
....
....
....
....
....
....

Day 2 Can a person truly think about their own thoughts in a meaningful way? When was the last time you took time to try to do this?

....
....
....
....
....
....
....
....
....
....
....
....
....
....
....
....
....
....
....
....

Day 3 What are "nettles" in this passage? What types of nettles are likely to overrun your mind?

....

....

....

....

....

....

....

....

....

....

....

....

....

....

....

....

....

....

....

Day 4 Think of some things this week that have entered your mind that you would rather not think about. Where did these thoughts come from?

....

....

....

....

....

....

....

....

....

....

....

....

....

....

....

....

....

....

....

Day 5 Have you encountered people this week whom you think have not "weeded" their minds lately? What was it like dealing with such individuals?

....
....
....
....
....
....
....
....
....
....
....
....
....
....
....
....
....
....
....

Day 6 How would you know that you need to take time to clear your mind of negative thoughts? What have you experienced this week that needs to be cleared away?

....
....
....
....
....
....
....
....
....
....
....
....
....
....
....
....
....
....
....

Day 7 When people do take time to weed their minds, what is the result? What is the result for you?

....

....

....

....

....

....

....

....

....

....

....

....

....

....

....

....

....

....

....

....

Day 1 Take a moment to look at the painting. How does it make you feel? What do you like the most about it?

....
....
....
....
....
....
....
....
....
....
....
....

Day 2 Look closely at it again. Where is the father in this family? What factors influenced your response?

....

....

....

....

....

....

....

....

....

....

....

....

....

....

....

....

....

....

....

....

ay 3 Did you find the man in the shadows? Why do
ou think he is in the shadows?

....

....

....

....

....

....

....

....

....

....

....

....

....

....

....

....

....

....

....

....

Day 4 When do you feel like you are in the shadows? What in your life makes you feel left out?

....

....

....

....

....

....

....

....

....

....

....

....

....

....

....

....

....

....

....

....

Day 5 Write a short story about this family. Who are they? Where do they live?

....

....

....

....

....

....

....

....

....

....

....

....

....

....

....

....

....

....

....

....

....

Day 6 If you could be anyone in this painting, whom would you be and why?

....
....
....
....
....
....
....
....
....
....
....
....
....
....
....
....
....
....

ay 7 Does this scene remind you of an event or story in your own life? Describe that time. Do you feel the same way about that time in your life as you do about the painting?

....

....

....

....

....

....

....

....

....

....

....

....

....

....

....

....

....

....

....

"Either the well was very deep, or she fell very slowly, for she had plenty of time as she went down to look about her, and to wonder what was going to happen next... Down, down, down. Would the fall never come to an end?"

Day 1 What is your initial reaction to this passage?

....

....

....

....

....

....

....

....

....

....

....

....

....

....

Day 2 Have you ever felt like you were an observer in your own life? When? What was it like?

....

....

....

....

....

....

....

....

....

....

....

....

....

....

....

....

....

....

....

....

....

Day 3 Describe a time this week when you felt as though you were moving in a certain direction without knowing where you would end up.

....

....

....

....

....

....

....

....

....

....

....

....

....

....

....

....

....

....

....

Day 4 Create a character that may have made these statements. Write a short description of him or her.

....

....

....

....

....

....

....

....

....

....

....

....

....

....

....

....

....

....

....

Day 5 Looking back at Day 4, do you relate to the character you created? Why or why not?

....

....

....

....

....

....

....

....

....

....

....

....

....

....

....

....

....

....

....

....

Day 6 Is this statement a happy one or a depressing one? Why?

....
....
....
....
....
....
....
....
....
....
....
....
....
....
....
....
....
....
....
....
....

Day 7 Think back on your week thus far. Would you have chosen to experience what you've gone through even if you didn't always know the outcome? Why?

....

....

....

....

....

....

....

....

....

....

....

....

....

....

....

This past year has been kind of a fall, or journey, into the unknown. Reflect on your comfort level with delving into unknown places within yourself.

Month Twelve

"The vacant mind is ever on the watch for relief, and ready to plunge into error, to escape from the languor of idleness. Store it with ideas, teach it the pleasure of thinking; and the temptations of the world without will be counteracted by the gratifications derived from the world within."

Day 1 What does this passage mean to you? What about it encourages you? What discourages you?

....

....

....

....

....

....

....

....

....

....

....

....

....

Day 2 Do you ever feel like your mind is "vacant"? How does this make you feel?

....

....

....

....

....

....

....

....

....

....

....

....

....

....

....

....

....

....

....

....

Day 3 Read this passage again. Why is a vacant mind dangerous?

....

....

....

....

....

....

....

....

....

....

....

....

....

....

....

....

....

....

....

....

Day 4 How do you see your "world without" versus you "world within"? Which would you rather live in and why?

....

....

....

....

....

....

....

....

....

....

....

....

....

....

....

....

....

....

....

Day 5 What are some of the things you would like to store your mind with? Write those things down. Are you surprised by your response?

....

....

....

....

....

....

....

....

....

....

....

....

....

....

....

....

....

....

....

....

....

Day 6 What are some of the temptations of the world that muddle your mind? Are these things different after a year of daily journal writing?

....
....
....
....
....
....
....
....
....
....
....
....
....
....
....
....
....
....
....
....

Day 7 How did writing down both happy and sad thoughts change your mood? Is this a worthwhile exercise?

....

....

....

....

....

....

....

....

....

....

....

....

....

....

....

....

....

....

....

....

....

Day 1 What is your initial reaction to this painting? Take 2 minutes to write down your thoughts.

....

....

....

....

....

....

....

....

....

....

....

....

Day 2 Is there beauty in this picture? Where?

....

....

....

....

....

....

....

....

....

....

....

....

....

....

....

....

....

....

....

....

Day 3 What scares you about this picture? Why?

....

....

....

....

....

....

....

....

....

....

....

....

....

....

....

....

....

....

....

....

Day 4 Which eyes caught your attention first, the full eyes or the empty ones? Why?

....
....
....
....
....
....
....
....
....
....
....
....
....
....
....
....
....
....
....
....
....
....

Day 5 Have you felt this week like you were being watched? When?

....

....

....

....

....

....

....

....

....

....

....

....

....

....

....

....

....

....

....

....

Day 6 If this many eyes were focused on you, what would they notice?

....

....

....

....

....

....

....

....

....

....

....

....

....

....

....

....

....

....

....

....

....

Day 7 If this many eyes were focused on you, what do you wish they would notice? How does this differ from your answer to Day 6?

....
....
....
....
....
....
....
....
....
....
....
....
....
....
....
....
....

If you have a negative reaction to the partial human form, it may mean you have unfinished business within your own interpersonal relationships.

"And afterward I will tell of our journey, and all the remnant of our pilgrimage. But first of your courtesy I pray you that ye ascribe it not to my rudeness in this narrative, though I speak plainly in telling you their words and their cheer; nor though I speak their very words."

Day 1 What comes to mind when you read this passage? Though it is clearly from a different era, does it hold modern themes?

....

....

....

....

....

....

....

....

....

....

....

....

....

Day 2 Does warning someone that you are going to be offensive make it okay to speak rudely? Has this happened to you?

....

....

....

....

....

....

....

....

....

....

....

....

....

....

....

....

....

....

....

....

Day 3 When was the last time someone relayed an experience of yours that was not exactly true? Is this the same as gossip?

....
....
....
....
....
....
....
....
....
....
....
....
....
....
....
....
....
....
....

Day 4 Is it better to speak plainly even if it might hurt someone's feelings? Have you been caught in this situation recently?

....

....

....

....

....

....

....

....

....

....

....

....

....

....

....

....

....

....

....

....

Day 5 Create a character who might have said this. Does he or she relate to someone in your life?

....
....
....
....
....
....
....
....
....
....
....
....
....
....
....
....
....
....
....
....

Day 6 Think back on your week. Have you been on the receiving end of someone speaking plainly to you without regard for your feelings? If not recently, when was the last time this happened?

....

....

....

....

....

....

....

....

....

....

....

....

....

....

....

....

....

....

Day 7 Is it rude to tell stories about other people and put your own spin on it? When was the last time you did this?

....

....

....

....

....

....

....

....

....

....

....

....

....

....

....

....

> *Speaking plainly may make us uncomfortable, but if we have moments of purity in thought and expression, we learn a great deal about our inner workings.*

Final Summary

Day 1 Look at your entries for Month 1. Now look at Month 12. How do they differ? How have you grown?

....

....

....

....

....

....

....

....

....

....

....

....

....

....

Day 2 As you became more comfortable with "reading" the literature and art, which do you find more engaging? What does this tell you about yourself?

....

....

....

....

....

....

....

....

....

....

....

....

....

....

....

....

....

....

....

Day 3 How do you think these exercises affect the way you approach circumstances in your own life?

....

....

....

....

....

....

....

....

....

....

....

....

....

....

....

....

....

....

....

....

Day 4 How do you think these exercises affect the way you approach or deal with others around you?

....
....
....
....
....
....
....
....
....
....
....
....
....
....
....
....
....
....
....
....
....
....

Day 5 What has been the most helpful tool you have learned this year?

....
....
....
....
....
....
....
....
....
....
....
....
....
....
....
....
....
....
....

Day 6 Thinking hard, and being totally honest with yourself, list ten things that you would like to improve about yourself and the way you handle your reactions to the world around you.

....

....

....

....

....

....

....

....

....

....

....

....

....

....

....

....

....

....

....

Day 7 Now list ten things about yourself and the way you approach life that make you pleased and that you would want to share with others. Post these ten things where you can see them every day and be proud of yourself for your new insights. You've earned it!

....

....

....

....

....

....

....

....

....

....

....

....

....

....

....

....

....

Bibliography

Title Page
    Bath Pathway, Andrea Michelle Napier

Month One
    Week 1 – *Obstructed View of Bath,* Andrea Michelle Napier
    Week 2 – *Macbeth*, William Shakespeare
    Week 3 – *Abandoned*, Max Klinger
    Week 4 – *Gone With the Wind*, Margaret Mitchell

Month Two
    Week 1 – *Vinyard Patio*, Andrea Michelle Napier
    Week 2 – *Dracula*, Bram Stoker
    Week 3 – *Group on a Balcony*, Francisco Goya
    Week 4 – *Sonnet 116*, William Shakespeare

Month Three
    Week 1 – *Moulin de la Galette,* Auguste Renoir
    Week 2 – *Brave New World*, Aldous Huxley
    Week 3 – *On the Balcony*, Berthe Morisot

Month Four
    Week 1 – *Charleston House*, Andrea Michelle Napier
    Week 2 – *A Farwell to Arms*, Ernest Hemingway
    Week 3 – *Lady Hamilton as Serena Reading A Newspaper*, George Romney
    Week 4 – *Persuasion*, Jane Austen

Month Five
    Week 1 – *Fauna in La Mancha*, Vladimir Kush
    Week 2 – *A Sentimental Journey*, Laurence Stern
    Week 3 – *Wheatfields*, Jacob Van Ruisdael
    Week 4 – *Where I Lived and What I Lived For*, Henry David Thoreau

Month Six
    Week 1 – *Alley in Charleston*, Andrea Michelle Napier
    Week 2 – *Sense and Sensibility*, Jane Austen
    Week 3 – *Satan Before the Throne of God* by William Blake

Month Seven
    Week 1 – *Self Portrait with Cigarette*, Edvard Munch
    Week 2 – *Frankenstein*, Mary Shelley
    Week 3 – *Wine is a Mocker*, Jan Steen
    Week 4 – *Songs of Innocence and Experience*, William Blake

Month Eight
    Week 1 – *Two Strings To Her Bow*, John-Pettie
    Week 2 – *Paradise Lost*, John Milton
    Week 3 – *View of Delft*, Vermeer
    Week 4 – *The Heart of Darkness*, Joseph Conrad

Month Nine
    Week 1 – *The Last of England*, Maddox Brown
    Week 2 – *Great Expectations*, Charles Dickens
    Week 3 – *Stormy Mountains*, Andrea Michelle Napier

Month Ten
    Week 1 – *Two Women Reading*, Pablo Picasso
    Week 2 – *Ode a Cassandre*, Pierre de Ronsard
    Week 3 – *Denial of St. Peter,* Caravaggio
    Week 4 – *A Sentimental Journey*, Laurence Sterne

Month Eleven
    Week 1 – *Milk Maid*, Vermeer
    Week 2 – *To Lady Allesbury*, Horace Walpole
    Week 3 – *One of the Family*, Frederick G. Cotman
    Week 4 – *Alice in Wonderland*, Lewis Carroll

Month Twelve
    Week 1 – *The Mysteries of Udolpho*, Ann Radcliffe
    Week 2 – *Eyes*, Salvador Dali
    Week 3 – *The Canterbury Tales*, Chaucer